As one of the world's longest established
and best-known travel brands,
Thomas Cook are the experts in travel.

For more than 135 years our
guidebooks have unlocked the secrets
of destinations around the world,
sharing with travellers a wealth of
experience and a passion for travel.

**Rely on Thomas Cook as your
[...] your next trip
[...] nique heritage.**

G000162533

Thomas Cook **pocket** guides

EXETER

Thomas
Cook

Your travelling companion since 1873

Written by Debbie Stowe

Published by Thomas Cook Publishing
A division of Thomas Cook Tour Operations Limited
Company registration no. 3772199 England
The Thomas Cook Business Park, Unit 9, Coningsby Road,
Peterborough PE3 8SB, United Kingdom
Email: books@thomascook.com, Tel: +44 (0) 1733 416477
www.thomascookpublishing.com

Produced by Cambridge Publishing Management Limited
Burr Elm Court, Main Street, Caldecote CB23 7NU
www.cambridgepm.co.uk

ISBN: 978-1-84848-467-2

This first edition © 2011 Thomas Cook Publishing
Text © Thomas Cook Publishing
Cartography supplied by Redmoor Design, Tavistock, Devon
Map data © OpenStreetMap contributors CC-BY-SA, www.openstreetmap.org,
www.creativecommons.org

Series Editor: Karen Beaulah
Production/DTP: Steven Collins

Printed and bound in Spain by GraphyCems

Cover photography © Thomas Cook Publishing

CONTENTS

SYMBOLS KEY

The following symbols are used throughout this book:

a address **t** telephone **w** website address **e** email
c opening times **N** public transport connections **!** important

The following symbols are used on the maps:

i information office   O   city
✈ airport   O   large town
+ hospital   o   small town
⬟ police station   =   motorway
▣ bus station   —   main road
▤ railway station   —   minor road
✝ cathedral   —   railway
    point of interest
1 numbers denote featured cafés, restaurants & venues

PRICE CATEGORIES

The ratings below indicate average price rates for a double room per night, including breakfast:
£ under £40   ££ £40–80   £££ over £80
The typical cost for a three-course meal without drinks is as follows:
£ under £12   ££ £12–20   £££ over £20

▶ *The magnificent West Front of St Peter's Cathedral*

INTRODUCING
Exeter

Introduction

Set in the midst of the rolling hills of Devon and with two of Britain's great wildernesses on its doorstep, the county town of Exeter would be highly unlikely to be a frenetic metropolitan blur. Few cities are more laid-back: for the picnickers outside the cathedral, the ducks on the quay or the shoppers ambling around Princesshay and Gandy Street, the default pace seems to be leisurely, encapsulating a relaxed urban Englishness.

Much of Exeter's atmosphere comes from the comforting authority of **St Peter's Cathedral**. This landmark building exudes Gothic majesty, and its grandeur truly is awe-inspiring. But this astonishing architectural accomplishment is just one of the city's many historical legacies. **Guildhall**, the country's oldest functioning civic building, joins half a dozen medieval churches to confer a real sense of a living past on the town. Factor in the occasional cobbled street and quirky attractions such as the 14th-century **Parliament Street** – the narrowest in Britain – and the thrilling **Underground Passages**, and the olde-worlde ambience is rounded off in style.

None of which is to say that Exeter is stuck in the past. On the contrary, its student population and tourist trade have been the engine of significant forward thinking. The city is home to some exuberantly modern attractions, epitomised by the tremendous **Exeter Phoenix** arts centre. Culturally and nocturnally, Exeter effervesces, with top events venues, hip clubs, first-rate restaurants and an active festival calendar. Its fusion of old and new is best summed up by **The Quay**, where the historical port now hosts a scintillating café culture and night scene.

To top all this, the city's highlights are so compactly spaced that it's quite easy to see pretty well everything on foot. However, should you get itchy feet and decide to stray beyond the town's boundaries, the wild magnetism of **Dartmoor National Park** and the cheery beach resorts of the **South Devon coast** lie within easy striking distance. Little wonder that Exeter numbers no less distinguished a fan than Charles Dickens among the many repeat visitors in its history.

The fine stained-glass window and oak-beamed roof of Exeter's Guildhall

When to go

SEASONS & CLIMATE

England's southwest peninsula, on which Exeter is situated, enjoys some of the warmest weather in the British Isles (which, admittedly, is not necessarily saying an awful lot!). Although anyone who turns up expecting reliably Mediterranean-type conditions will be disappointed, the sun does assert itself in this part of the world to some extent throughout the year. As is the case around the country, the hottest period is July and August (which also suffer the least precipitation), and the coldest January and February, with monthly temperatures gradually changing between the two extremes.

However, the best time of year for the weather is logically also the busiest for tourism, coinciding with the school holidays, which bring families flocking to the beaches of Devon and the adjacent county, Cornwall. While Exeter itself is not a big hub for holidaymakers and second-home owners, it does see some regional overspill, and the resulting traffic congestion in the vicinity can be a nuisance, so it can be worth timing your trip to be just outside peak season. Winter visitors should be prepared for British levels of cold. Whenever you come, there's a fair chance of rain.

ANNUAL EVENTS

Exeter boasts a respectable cultural calendar for a city of its size. The quirky film fest **Animated Exeter** (ⓦ www.animatedexeter.co.uk) is held in mid-February. Then, for a couple of weeks in March, the strains of music – jazz, blues,

funk, soul, world, hip-hop and R & B among other genres –
waft through the city during the **Vibraphonic Festival**
( www.2020vibraphonic.co.uk). From late June until some time
in mid-July, the **Exeter Summer Festival** features music, dance,
theatre, comedy and exhibitions, while the correspondingly
named **Exeter Autumn Festival**, generally held during the first
two weeks of November, is a similarly arts- and literature-based
event, with a focus on encouraging and developing local talent.
At about the same time of year **Exeter Open Studios**
(www.exeteropenstudios.co.uk) sees artists welcome the
public into their workshops to witness and discuss the
creative process.

◔ *Springtime in Exeter: magnolia trees in bloom*

History

Exeter first popped up appreciably on the historical radar in Roman times, although it was previously an Iron Age settlement and its roots are probably Celtic. The discovery of coins from the period suggests that the spot was something of a commercial hub – little surprise considering its favourable riverside location – but the departure of the 5,000 Romans stationed here sent it into decline. Nonetheless, the significant vestiges of the Roman stay, when the city was the regional capital of the Southwest, conferred infrastructure that allowed the conquering Saxons to cohabit with the defeated Britons from the 7th century. But medieval Exeter, then one of the country's largest towns, had a chequered time of things. Between the 9th and the 11th

⬤ *The old Exe Bridge was constructed in the 13th century*

centuries the city was variously in the control of the Danes, Alfred the Great, King Athelstan and Emma of Normandy.

The unrest continued after the Battle of Hastings in 1066. Defiant Exeter rose up against William the Conqueror, who reasserted his authority through a siege. He then built **Rougemont Castle**, following the city's honourable surrender, to preclude any repeat of the insubordination. Although that did not spell the end of the upheaval, in the late Middle Ages some commerce began to establish itself, with markets and fairs becoming a more productive and stable part of city life.

Exeter's commercial contribution continued into the Tudor and Stuart periods, and its donation of ships helped the country to triumph against the Spanish Armada in 1588. By the time of the English Civil War (1642–51), the city was doing a thriving international trade in wool, employing thousands of people and producing several types of cloth.

It wasn't to last. As steam power edged waterways out of the picture, Exeter's distance from a coal source meant it couldn't compete with the industrialised mills of northern England, and it took a back seat in British industry, although nearby canals kept the local economy going. While Victorian industrialisation did not scar the city, the German Luftwaffe did, in World War II, with devastating aerial bombardment. Between the historical buildings that survived or were repaired, much of the town's architecture is more modern in style. Today's Exeter is characterised by a lively university population and a decent tourist infrastructure that has given Devon's county town a fresh identity as a pleasant urban stop-off for visitors to England's southwest peninsula.

Culture

Despite its relatively small proportions, Exeter punches well above its weight culturally. The city possesses a remarkable literary gem: the 10th-century **_Exeter Book_**, preserved in the vaults of the cathedral, contains rare examples of Old English poetry.

The sizeable student population keeps a vibrant cultural scene ticking over, in the form of various festivals, arts venues and museums, and with an emphasis on the niche rather than the mainstream. The university is actively involved in Exeter's cultural life; the **Bill Douglas Centre**, located on the campus, contains a vast collection of artefacts relating to the history of film.

The theatre is particularly well represented in the city, with two main venues backed up by an impressive supporting cast of smaller, independent operations. Regular events include an annual Shakespeare performance in the grounds of Rougemont Castle.

Music also pervades city life, not only through the Exeter Festival and the Vibraphonic Festival but also through the smattering of backstreet bars and clubs that showcase live performances away from the main streets. Coldplay lead singer Chris Martin is probably Exeter's highest-profile musical export.

Cultural goings-on are detailed in several guides and magazines, and on websites, including that of Exeter City Council (Ⓦ www.exeter.gov.uk).

▶ _Half-timbered houses in Exeter High Street_

MAKING THE MOST OF
Exeter

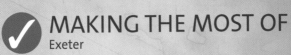

Shopping

Retail opportunities in Exeter run the usual UK gamut from the stock high-street names and malls to quirkier, independent outlets. The former are concentrated on and around, naturally enough, the city's High Street and interconnecting roads. The undercover **Harlequins Shopping Centre** offers the modern mall experience, while the interlinked **Guildhall Shopping Centre**, an attractive old building that dates from the 13th century, dishes up more of the same but with a historical ambience.

Pedestrianised **Princesshay** is another pleasantly 'period' retail district, whose atmosphere comes in large part from Roman Walk and the visible sections of the city wall. It is partially covered, although still with an outside feel, and public art features add to the charm of the area.

Bohemian and alternative shoppers are catered for on **Castle Street** and the narrow, cobbled **Gandy Street**, while the area surrounding the cathedral is home to more traditional outlets. Art, jewellery and designer boutiques are among the businesses plying their wares in these parts. **Fore Street** plays host to a gaggle of retro and second-hand clothing stores, and other left-field emporiums.

Devon enjoys a thriving market tradition. A farmers' market is held on Thursdays at Fore Street's corner with **South Street** (☎ 01392 665480 ⏰ 09.00–14.00). The same spot is the scene of a monthly craft market in the warmer months. **Sidwell Street Market** purveys clothes, accessories, plants and various other items.

Away from the town centre, **The Quay** provides pleasant waterside shopping, with gift and craft stores and watersports outlets predominating.

Exeter does not have an obvious archetypal product associated with it, but foodie Devon is at the vanguard of the UK's organic farming movement, so some local consumables could serve as a tasty memento of your visit.

In general, prices are much the same as across the country, although the more tourist-oriented shops tend to charge a premium. ⓦ www.exetershopping.org

🔺 *From trendsetter to bohemian, all shoppers are catered for*

Eating & drinking

England's entire southwest peninsula has very much embraced the country's new gastronomic trends and, as an open-minded city, Exeter is a happy beneficiary. The town has some top-quality restaurants, drawing on the organic and local principles espoused by the 21st-century ethical foodie. Its location – amid fertile farmland and not far from the coast – provides the raw ingredients for a smorgasbord of delightful dishes.

The culinary ethos is showcased at the annual **Exeter Festival of South West Food & Drink**, as well as at smaller-scale **farmers' markets**. Edibles on the table range from traditional pub lunches to highly sophisticated multi-course meals in top eateries, such as the splendidly located Michael Caines at ABode restaurant. A hungry-yet-impecunious student demographic also ensures plenty of cheap eats.

If you're after a quintessential eating experience, a good option is the Devonshire cream tea, which typically consists of a pot of tea with scones that are eaten with cream (usually clotted, sometimes whipped) and jam. As with many such flagship regional staples, the precise serving instructions and origins are taken rather seriously, although local restaurateurs are usually more relaxed. The cream comes from the county's farms, which also yield up acclaimed ice cream, lamb and venison. Although it's not specific to Devon, the British Sunday lunch, served in many local pubs, is another satisfyingly calorific tradition.

Despite its city status, Exeter has a streak of provincialism and there is little tradition of late-night dining. Beyond about

21.00 or 22.00, your restaurant choice will diminish dramatically. Cafés, too, all tend to shut up shop by around 18.00, sometimes even slightly earlier, although some chains may operate for an extra hour or so.

If the weather is good, the outside tables down at atmospheric Exeter Quay are thronged with diners and drinkers. Cathedral Close is another top spot if you'd like your meal or snack set off by a superlative view.

● *Enjoy fresh local produce from the farmers' markets*

Entertainment

It would be difficult to get bored in Exeter as the city successfully caters for the leisure proclivities of both its resident students and the incoming tourist. Its nocturnal scene is vigorous and varied. Trendy clubs, relaxed lounge bars and traditional venues all compete for the reveller's attention after dark, with many staging live music and events. Local listings magazines can help you to pick a place likely to suit, or you can simply wander around the town centre until your visual or aural interest is piqued. **The Quay** is something of a nightlife hub on the long summer evenings, although its pull wanes a little in winter.

St Peter's Cathedral is the stunning setting for a range of events, from organ recitals and symphony concerts to choral evenings and poetry readings.

Several mainstream venues stage concerts, and the welcoming, modern and innovative **Exeter Phoenix** venue hosts a wide-ranging programme featuring niche and alternative films, music and performance.

There are two main theatres – **Northcott** (located on the university campus) and **Barnfield** (which hosts some amateur productions) – neither of which restricts itself to drama. Ballet, opera, stand-up comedy, children's shows, tribute bands and even puppetry also pop up on What's On lists.

All the major venues have well-maintained websites, while the tourist information office, Exeter City Council website, and various listings sites and magazines also provide specifics of forthcoming events. The Exeter List (ⓦ www.exeterlist.co.uk) is one such site, giving details of local goings-on in an assortment of categories.

▲ *Enjoy an evening's entertainment in the magnificent St Peter's Cathedral*

Sport & relaxation

Given the wealth of natural beauty within easy reach of the city and the often clement (again, by UK standards) weather, a stay in Exeter provides the opportunity for some wonderful outdoor recreation. Although the city is not on the coast, watersports take place in the canal basin at Exeter Quay. The town also serves as a useful base from which to organise a host of aquatic pursuits. Canoeing, surfing, diving and – at the lower-tech end of the scale – swimming are popular pastimes on the nearby beaches. The rolling Devon hills and both Dartmoor and Exmoor national parks are also ripe for exploring, whether on foot, on a bike or on one of the quintessential moorland ponies.

Cyclists are well catered for. Cutely named **Saddles & Paddles** is a bike and canoe hire outlet that sells and services cycles as well. ⓐ 4 Kings Wharf, The Quay ⓣ 01392 424241 ⓦ www.sadpad.com ⓛ 08.30–18.00 (summer); 09.00–17.00 (winter)

The **Bike Shed** also sells cycles and accessories. ⓐ 163 Fore Street, opposite Walkabout in alley ⓣ 01392 426196 ⓦ www.bikesheduk.com ⓛ 08.30–17.30 Mon–Wed & Fri, 08.30–20.00 Thur, 09.00–17.30 Sat, 10.00–16.00 Sun

To approach the national parks in a more structured way, consult the relevant tourist authority (ⓦ www.dartmoor-npa.gov.uk or ⓦ www.exmoor-nationalpark.gov.uk); these websites have an abundance of information on potential walking routes and activities.

If hiking up hill and down dale or getting wet and wild with some watersports sounds too energetic for you, a more sedate and serene option is to proceed to one of the spas springing up in the city, either in the more upmarket hotels or as stand-alone operations.

Alternatively, if you prefer to watch others do the running, head to St James Park, home of Exeter City Football Club (ⓦ www.exetercityfc.co.uk) on match day. They may not have the cachet of a Premier League outfit but, after successive promotions, the team is riding high, and a league match could provide a pleasant afternoon out.

🔺 *Explore the river by ferry or paddle power*

Accommodation

Geared-up Exeter has a cross-section of places to lay your head, from expensive hotels to less costly lodgings such as bed & breakfasts, university accommodation (during the summer and Easter holidays), hostels and campsites – although you'll have to travel a little way out of town for the latter. Many of the B & Bs are clustered in the suburban streets close to the two train stations. Exeter doesn't stage the kind of massive event that sees all accommodation snapped up, and therefore if you turn up on spec, you may be in luck; but, as might be expected, weekends and bank holidays over the summer and the school holidays are likely to see more demand than weekdays in midwinter, so if you're planning to travel at peak times, it is wise to book a room or bed.

Axe Hayes Farm £ This affable campsite, with decent facilities following a recent refurbishment, lies 3.25 km (2 miles) to the east of town. Another nearby site, **Hill Pond £** (☏ 01392 232483), operates in the warmer months. ⓐ Sidmouth Road, Clyst St Mary ☏ 01395 232336 Ⓝ Bus: 52A, 52B

Globe Backpackers £ This is a fun and friendly hostel run by experienced travellers who know what the backpacker wants. Located in an 18th-century townhouse, the premises are clean and comfortable. Beds are mostly bunks in dorm rooms, but there's also a double room with a four-poster if you yearn for a touch more privacy or luxury. ⓐ 71 Holloway Street ☏ 01392 215521 Ⓦ www.exeterbackpackers.co.uk

University of Exeter £ Penny-wise University of Exeter makes nifty use of its vacant accommodation when the students depart for Easter and the summer by letting out rooms to visitors. B & B and room-only accommodation is available on the verdant Streatham Campus, while the smaller St Luke's Campus in Heavitree Road offers B & B only. Use of the sports facilities is a bonus. ⓐ Reed Hall, Streatham Drive ☏ 01392 215566 ⓦ www.exeter.ac.uk ⓝ Bus: D (Streatham Campus); Bus: H (St Luke's Campus)

Georgian Lodge ££ Located in a pretty, pale yellow, Grade II listed town house, this intimate hotel has ten en-suite rooms and Wi-Fi Internet throughout the property. Prices include a full English or continental breakfast. Part of a small chain, its three affiliates can be found at ⓐ 16 New North Road ⓐ 12 Queens Terrace and ⓐ 28 Alphington Road ⓐ 5 Bystock Terrace ☏ 01392 213079 ⓦ www.georgianlodge.com

Jurys Inn ££ For a good night's sleep at an affordable price, try the Exeter hotel in the good-value and unostentatious Jurys Inn chain. The tastefully decorated rooms are airy, comfortable and very quiet – despite the central location – and the staff maintain a low-key geniality. A great choice for the budget traveller. ⓐ Western Way ☏ 01392 312400 ⓦ www.exeterhotels.jurysinns.com

Raffles ££ This red-brick Victorian town house offers B & B accommodation in harmoniously furnished (the owners are also antiques dealers) en-suite rooms. It is situated in the centre of

town, but off-street parking is available. ⓐ 11 Blackall Road
ⓣ 01392 270200 ⓦ www.raffles-exeter.co.uk

White Hart Hotel ££ This is billed as one of Exeter's most historic
inns: guests – originally monks – have been recharging their
batteries here for about seven centuries. The property now hosts
55 rooms, although the majority are in an extension rather than
the historical bit. Some are done out to complement the
surrounding history, others reflect a more modern sensibility,
while all are en-suite. ⓐ 66 South Street ⓣ 01392 279897
ⓦ www.whitehartpubexeter.co.uk

Bendene ££–£££ The outside swimming pool is the big surprise
at this well-priced and central town-house B & B. Rooms are
divided between en-suite and cheaper accommodation with a
shared bathroom. There's also free Wi-Fi access. The building has
five floors and no lift, so if you have mobility issues, ask in
advance to be housed on the ground floor or a low floor.
ⓐ 15–16 Richmond Road ⓣ 01392 254162
ⓦ www.bendene.co.uk

ABode Exeter £££ The ABode Exeter has taken over the premises
of the Royal Clarence, said to be the country's first-ever hotel.
The grand, pillared entrance, presided over by a coat of arms,
heralds the luxury that guests can expect, which includes 'Vi-
Spring beds' and 'monsoon showers'. Throw in the unbeatable
location and it will become clear why staying here costs that
little bit extra. ⓐ Cathedral Yard ⓣ 01392 319955
ⓦ www.abodehotels.co.uk/exeter

Mercure £££ Flagging up its claimed status as the only hotel in Exeter with a swimming pool and gym, the four-star Mercure also enjoys a quiet yet central position. Following a takeover by French hotel group Accor, the 154 rooms have been upgraded and now reflect a stylish and contemporary French vibe. The swanky lobby, replete with grandiose mirrors, also wows.
ⓐ Southernhay East ⓣ 01392 412812 ⓦ www.mercure.com

Rougemont Hotel by Thistle £££ Those rooms that have been recently refurbished are characterised by sleek and stylish lines, while the rest are more traditional in feel, at this welcoming and helpful four-star hotel. The rooms, which come with complimentary magazines and toiletries, are categorised as standard, de luxe and executive. There is wireless Internet access throughout the property. ⓐ Queen Street ⓣ 0871 376 9018
ⓦ www.thistle.com

St Olaves Hotel £££ This two-centuries-old Georgian town house is marvellously traditional in atmosphere, with a selection of modern and period-style accommodation. The 15 rooms, two of which are suites, are individually decorated with exquisite taste, and are furnished with tea, coffee and home-made biscuits. Service is polite, discreet and welcoming.
ⓐ Mary Arches Street ⓣ 01392 217736 ⓦ www.olaves.co.uk

THE BEST OF EXETER

From the ancient architecture to the up-to-the-minute cultural scene, there's plenty of competition for your time and attention in the city.

TOP 10 ATTRACTIONS

- **St Peter's Cathedral** A grand Gothic masterpiece, completed in the 14th century, that dominates the city (see pages 49–50).

- **The Quay** This picturesque area is steeped in history, but its cosy cafés, cutting-edge clubs and laid-back terraces are right up to date (see pages 71–2).

- **Guildhall** The country's oldest working civic building, surveyed imperiously by a bust of Queen Victoria, emanates stately dignity (see page 45).

- **Underground Passages** Scrabbling around in Britain's only medieval tunnel network open to visitors is a superb subterranean adventure (see pages 62–3).

- **Exeter Phoenix** A unique and exciting cultural venue where dance, drama, DJ sets, art, film and food come together in a fabulous location (see page 64).

- **Devonshire cream tea** It might be a diet-buster, but sampling the county's archetypal afternoon snack is a genteel culinary reminder of old England (see page 16).

- **Dartmoor National Park** Leave the modern urban world behind and get truly back to nature in this ruggedly beautiful area (see pages 80–83).

- **Gandy Street** The cobbles of this charming, resolutely independent centre for the more bohemian shopper hark back to a bygone Exeter (see page 65).

- **Exciting nightlife** Whether you enjoy hanging out in a trendy bar or rocking to an up-and-coming band, Exeter has a venue for you (see pages 68, 78).

- **Northernhay Gardens** A verdant little oasis of urban tranquillity (see pages 58–9).

⬇ *The magnificent vaulted ceiling of St Peter's Cathedral*

Suggested itineraries

HALF-DAY: EXETER IN A HURRY

Exeter's compactness allows the visitor to pack in many of its top sights even on a fleeting visit. The must-see attraction is without doubt the cathedral and this should be your first destination. From here, Guildhall's proximity makes it worth popping in if it's open. Another top draw, especially if it's raining – although not for claustrophobes – are the Underground Passages. If the weather is fine, head south and enjoy lunch or dinner by the quay. Alternatively, Cathedral Close is also a picturesque spot for a bite.

1 DAY: TIME TO SEE A LITTLE MORE

With an entire day, the above circuit can be followed at a more leisurely pace. There will also be time to take in some culture. The revamped Royal Albert Memorial Museum (RAMM) will certainly be a top city sight when it reopens in late 2011. Close by, and also near the Underground Passages, is the terrific Exeter Phoenix arts centre. If there's an event on, this could provide you with your evening's entertainment too. Otherwise, try one of the theatres, or see if you can track down some live music.

2–3 DAYS: SHORT CITY-BREAK

With a couple of days or so at your disposal, you are now able to do Exeter in some depth. In addition to the highlights mentioned above, you can visit some of the city's churches, many of which are close to the cathedral. Rougemont Castle also deserves a look, and on this undemanding timescale you can also fit in some relaxation, in Northernhay and Rougemont gardens to the north and, across the other side of the city, at The Quay. Slightly less central attractions, such as the Bill Douglas Centre, also become more practical. And there is time to have your fill of the nightlife and culture, taking in a play or a show, live music and/or a club night, depending on your preferences.

LONGER: ENJOYING EXETER TO THE FULL

If you can devote even longer to your Exeter sojourn, both the city itself and its surroundings really open up to you. There'll be time for every city sight that appeals to you, and venues with a varied programme of events and exhibits, such as the Exeter Phoenix arts centre, may even merit a repeat visit. Consult the cathedral programme – a concert there is a special experience. Trips to Dartmoor and the nearby seaside towns will provide a rewarding counterpoint to your city break.

🔺 *The Underground Passages provide an exciting attraction*

Something for nothing

Exeter has plenty of options for the frugal – a state of affairs perhaps influenced by its ample student population. Admission to the cathedral is free, although they suggest a donation, and of course taking in its awe-inspiring exterior also costs nothing. There is no charge for dropping into Guildhall, likewise cultural venues such as the Royal Albert Memorial Museum and the Exeter Phoenix arts centre.

Exeter's small size is well suited for walking. Exploring the narrow, atmospheric streets around and to the north of the cathedral is a great way to imbibe the city's atmosphere with no financial outlay. The Rougemont and Quay areas are both charming to wander, and both have benches should you wish to repose a while and admire the views. The Exeter City Council website (ⓦ www.exeter.gov.uk) devotes a page to cost-free activities; if you want a structured meander, for example, try a Red Coat guided tour or a self-guided walk, available from the Quay House Visitor Centre (see page 93). More energetic free outdoor fun can be had hiking on Dartmoor, or, if the sun's out, pack some sandwiches, jump on a bus and spend the day at a nearby beach.

When it rains

The short distances involved in getting between Exeter's chief points of interest mean that on a rainy day it's practicable to minimise exposure by scuttling from one to the other. The cathedral, Guildhall and a smattering of nearby churches lie slightly south of the RAMM, Exeter Phoenix arts centre and the Underground Passages. These last three in particular all provide outstanding options during inclement weather. The RAMM and the Exeter Phoenix are both crammed with so much to see that hours can easily pass by – and if the Phoenix is hosting an evening event, it's feasible to be there well after sundown. The Underground Passages are also enormously popular on wet days, so much so that it is wise to book ahead to guarantee your place on a tour.

A downpour can provide an excuse for some shopping. Princesshay, Harlequins Shopping Centre and the Guildhall Shopping Centre are all partially or entirely under cover, so can serve as retail refuges from the rain. Another alternative is to hole up in one of the eateries in Cathedral Close or Cathedral Yard and enjoy the dramatic views of the Gothic building being lashed by the elements.

On arrival

ARRIVING BY AIR, RAIL OR ROAD

Exeter's international airport is in Clyst Honiton, 6.5 km (4 miles) east of the city. Buses 56 and 379 – the cheapest way of getting into town – connect the airport with Exeter's bus station and St David's Station, taking just under three-quarters of an hour to the former and an additional ten minutes to the latter. Pay the driver upon boarding. Buses stop running early, with the last service leaving the airport at around 18.30. There is no railway station at the airport proper, the closest option being Pinhoe. Exeter Airport Taxis is the sole cab firm authorised to operate from the site; book ahead to have a vehicle waiting. Expect to pay upwards of £10 for the 15-minute journey. If you're travelling in a group of three or four, a cab ride can work out as better value than the bus. The airport is also home to a few car-hire outlets.

Visitors pitching up by train are most likely to find themselves at Exeter St David's, which receives services from London Paddington, London Waterloo (albeit fewer – and interestingly they depart in the opposite direction), Birmingham New Street and other local stations. The city's main terminus is a short distance from the town centre, on Bonhay Road, northwest of the main action. It's about a 20-minute walk into town, with some hills involved. If you're laden with luggage or a trudge doesn't appeal, the H1 and H2 buses go to the city centre, taking just five minutes, or you could change on to another train service bound for Exeter Central. Although the more conveniently located of the two main terminuses (as its name suggests), this station is smaller, but it does serve London Waterloo as well as a handful of regional destinations. It is situated on Queen Street, so all the main city attractions can be readily reached on foot from here. Taxi ranks are to be found outside both stations.

By car, Exeter is approached by the M5 if you're coming from the north, the A38/A380 from the south and the A30 from the east or west. Bus passengers are dropped off right in the heart of things, at the city's bus garage on Paris Street.

FINDING YOUR FEET

Laid-back and relatively small, Exeter is a straightforward city to find your way around, even if you're not used to the urban pace of life. The city centre is normally fairly crime free although, as elsewhere in the UK, visitors should be careful at night in the vicinity of pubs, bars and clubs. Drunken carousers can make their presence felt on the streets and, although very unlikely to impact on passers-by, such boorish displays could alarm the unsuspecting tourist. In the event of a late arrival, it is a good idea to take a taxi rather than wander around unknown areas after dark.

ORIENTATION

Apart from the odd outlying site, such as the Bill Douglas Centre or the Northcott Theatre, all of the main points of interest are centrally located in a zone that approximately corresponds to the area inside and just beyond the old city wall. Bordered at the top by Rougemont Castle and its surrounding gardens, and at the bottom by The Quay, all the sights are easily doable on foot.

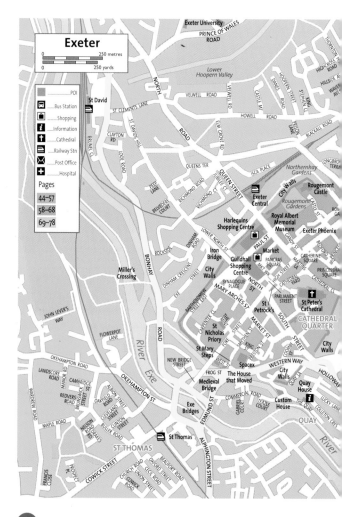

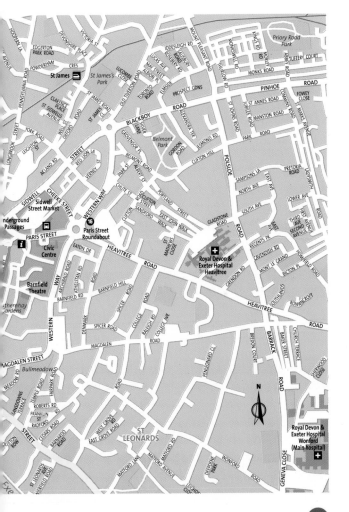

With the exception of getting to The Quay, when an incongruously busy road must be negotiated, Exeter is very much a walking city. Some of the main attractions are off-limits to cars, and even where vehicles are permitted, they tend to be few and relatively slow-moving.

The only potential fly in the orientation ointment is the lack of a widely visible landmark. Although the cathedral is large, it is not particularly tall, and the flanking town houses mean that it is feasible to be quite near St Peter's without actually being able to see the building itself. Neither is there any clock tower or tall, distinctive office block or hotel that can be consulted.

But getting around Exeter is not so confusing that this should present a problem. The spiritual heart of the place is St Peter's Cathedral, which sits proudly in the middle of grassy Cathedral Close. The area is set slightly back from the main thoroughfare that scythes through the city. Fore Street runs from southwest to northeast, later becoming the High Street and then Sidwell Street. Queen Street, a left turn shortly after Guildhall, is another useful road. Should you briefly lose your bearings, the council has erected a series of panels with city maps printed on them.

GETTING AROUND

The close proximity of its main sights allows the visitor to explore much of Exeter with little need for recourse to the public transport system. Should time be truly short, then the city's bus network, run principally by Stagecoach, may be of some use. If you're planning to zip around and make a lot of journeys in one day, a daily Explorer costing £5 offers good value.

⬥ *Cricklepit Suspension Bridge links the quayside with Haven Banks*

A regional version is available if your travels are going to take you further afield. Bus D might also come in handy for visiting the university campus. Tickets can be bought on board from the driver.

The bus is also likely to be your best bet if you're planning to see much of the surrounding area under your own steam. Routes that head out of the city mostly depart from the bus station on Paris Street. Services run between Exeter and the resorts on the south coast of Devon, including the 52 to Sidmouth and the 56 to Exmouth, for example. Buses also wend their way between the seaside resorts, allowing the visitor to tick off a few places in one fell swoop, or perhaps move on to the next town if one place doesn't appeal to them. Other services, including the 359 and 82, are also handy for getting over to Dartmoor.

A few of the nearby seaside towns, such as Exmouth, have their own station, so if you're planning on visiting just one resort, the train might be an option. While often faster, train travel tends to be slightly more expensive than the equivalent journey by bus. Journeys start from St David's or Central Station (and sometimes also the smaller, suburban station St Thomas, although that will be to little avail unless you happen to be staying in the area).

Apart from perhaps the airport run, the distances you'll need to cover in Exeter don't tend to merit taking a cab, but it's a good standby if you're particularly tired, the weather's rotten or it's late at night. Taxis in Exeter operate using much the same system as elsewhere in the UK. Numerous private cab firms are active in the city, with a car having to be booked by phone. Such

⬢ A bird's-eye view of Cathedral Close and the city

rides are typically cheaper than hackney cabs, the council-licensed vehicles that can be hailed in the street and also line up at ranks in busy places.

CAR HIRE

Although the attractions of Exeter itself, even the odd one outside the town centre, are readily done on foot, should you be intending to get out of the city and explore the beach resorts, or particularly the national parks, having access to your own vehicle will make things a lot easier. If you're flying in, several car-rental companies operate from the airport itself. The UK's major car-hire firms have bases either there or elsewhere in town, often on the Marsh Barton Trading Estate.

▶ *Rougemont Castle gatehouse*

THE CITY OF
Exeter

Introduction to city areas

Because of Exeter's size, any division of the city into separate areas is a fairly arbitrary process – unless you're planning your day with military efficiency – so it's quite easy to flit back and forth between the different parts of town delineated here.

The first section, **Around the cathedral**, covers the city's flagship building and the attractions scattered around it. This is where to head if time is so tight that you're only going to be able to stay for a couple of hours or so.

Still focusing within the city walls, the second section of the guide, **Around Rougemont**, moves north to what is probably Exeter's second most significant building, Rougemont Castle. Although the actual castle cannot be toured, it remains an important landmark and also sits in the vicinity of a clutch of other key sights, as well as some charming gardens.

The third section, **Outside the city walls**, covers everything outside the Roman perimeter – disparate highlights at The Quay, which is a short walk to the south of the city centre, and the Bill Douglas Centre, a rather lengthier trudge, or bus journey, to the north.

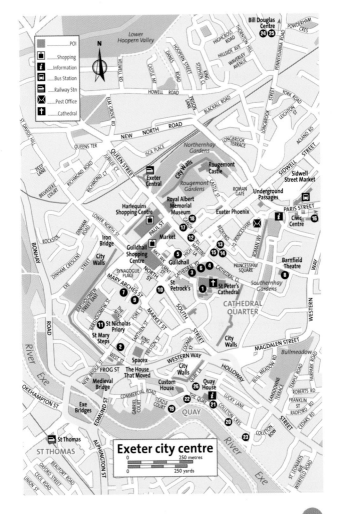

Exeter city centre

0 _____ 250 metres

0 _____ 250 yards

Around the cathedral

Exuding Gothic majesty, Exeter's top landmark, St Peter's
Cathedral, dominates the square in which it resides and sets
the tone for the surrounding area. The relative smallness of
the city serves only to exaggerate the building's striking
proportions. However, the cathedral is not visible from all over
town, meaning that if you emerge in front of it unexpectedly
from an alleyway it retains its power to awe. Running close by
the cathedral is the High Street. That street and the adjoining
ones also contain their fair complement of historical attractions
among the shops, which add to the refined atmosphere of
the area.

Unless your mobility is limited, walking is the best way to
get around this part of town. The series of 'you are here' maps
installed on all the main streets should ensure you do not lose
your way.

SIGHTS & ATTRACTIONS

Cathedral Quarter
Although dominated by one of Britain's most glorious
cathedrals, this area comprising Cathedral Yard and Cathedral
Close is a stylish and historical location in its own right.
Idiosyncratic half-timbered buildings line the square, with their
medley of period features ranging from medieval to Georgian.
The Elizabethan Mol's Coffee House – now a shoe and luggage
shop – is one of the most distinctive. Rest on a bench or sit on
the grass to admire the scene's charm.

Guildhall

The country's oldest working municipal building has an 850-year history that asserts itself from every fixture and fitting. Visitors enter through a stately Tudor portico, which leads to the main chamber. It is here that the city council still meets, under the austere gaze of a bust of Queen Victoria. Grand portraits of the great and the good, stained-glass windows and a beamed ceiling all add to the sense of being close to history. A genial mace sergeant is usually on hand to answer questions. A more

◆ *Book ahead to enjoy the historic Guildhall*

detailed guided tour, which also allows access to the jury room, cells, mayor's parlour, city regalia and silver balustrade can be arranged in advance. ⓐ High Street ⓣ 01392 665500 ⓦ www.exeter.gov.uk ⓛ Usually 10.30–13.00 & 14.00–16.00 Mon–Fri, 10.30–12.30 Sat, closed Sun, and also sometimes closed to the public on other days for mayoral functions; check ahead by phone, online or on the noticeboard outside

🔺 *Breathe in – narrow Parliament Street*

SMALL STREET, BIG INSULT

There is a subversive element to the history of Exeter's tiny Parliament Street. The narrow alleyway was previously called Small Lane. But when Exeter took exception to the 1832 Reform Bill brought in by Parliament, the name was changed as a sly dig at the House.

Parliament Street

An interesting contender in the series of quirky 'littlest' attractions up and down Britain, this dinky 14th-century cut-through, which links the High Street and Waterbeer Street, is said to be one of the world's narrowest streets (pipped to the title by a German competitor). Some 50 m (164 ft) long, at its widest it just exceeds 114 cm (45 in) and is squeezed to a tiny 64 cm (25 in) at its narrowest. ❸ Off High Street, southwest of Guildhall

St Mary Steps

Exeter is blessed with a surfeit of ancient churches, of which St Mary Steps is a particularly pretty example. A church has existed on the site since 1150, although what is in evidence today dates mainly from a 15th-century reconstruction. It is given a distinctive look by the use of red Heavitree sandstone, and the steep cobblestone path and steps alongside the building form a charmingly picturesque backdrop. The star feature is the Matthew the Miller clock, named after a 17th-century miller who regularly used to pass the site. Images signifying the four seasons, and a seated Henry VIII and two guards – who respectively nod and chime the bell on the hour – feature in the ornate design. The late Gothic nave is another highlight of the church. ⓐ West Street and Stepcote Hill ⓣ 01392 273530 (warders) ⓛ Open for services only

St Nicholas Priory

A taste of Tudor times is obtainable at this erstwhile guest wing of a Benedictine foundation and merchant's town house, which

◔ *St Mary Steps wind between attractive Tudor buildings*

has been refurnished as an Elizabethan home. The 900-year-old building features an array of architectural styles from over the centuries, visible in rooms on two floors. There is also a small collection of original artefacts. ⓐ The Mint, between Fore Street and Bartholomew Street West ① 01392 665858 ⓦ www.exeter.gov.uk ① 10.00–17.00 Mon–Sat (during local school holidays), except bank holidays, closed Sun; 10.00–17.00 Sat (during school term time), closed Sun–Fri ① Admission charge

St Peter's Cathedral

St Peter's is Exeter's most stirring edifice by a long way – and a staggering architectural feat. Although work was started on the building in the early 12th century by the Normans, extensive remodelling began a century and a half later and carried on for about another hundred years, which means that the dominant motifs are Decorated Gothic and Early English. External highlights include the two Norman towers, plus the intricate Gothic screen on the West Front, with its layers of sculpted figures, including King Alfred, William the Conqueror and Richard II – England's most extensive collection of 14th-century sculpture.

Inside, the cathedral is equally mesmerising. It contains the longest uninterrupted Gothic ceiling anywhere; as you crane your neck, look out for a depiction of the murder of Thomas à Becket among other adorned bulbous bosses. The astronomical clock, bearing the Latin motto *Pereunt et Imputantur* (a warning to spend one's limited time wisely), hefty organ and 13th-century misericords are among the numerous astonishing features. But besides the many visual wonders, part of the joy is merely drinking in the imposing atmosphere, perhaps best done if you manage to time your visit to coincide with a service or event, particularly when the choir is in action.

ⓐ 1 The Cloisters, Cathedral Yard ☎ 01392 255573
ⓦ www.exeter-cathedral.org.uk ⏱ Approximately 09.00–16.45 Mon–Sat, and for services, closed Sun except for services
ⓘ Admission free but suggested donation

St Petrock's

Another of Exeter's half-dozen medieval churches, this is noteworthy for an interior that has been described as being

ⵙ *The dazzling Anglican cathedral, St Peter's*

THE CATHEDRAL CLOCK

The clock in St Peter's Cathedral is said by some – perhaps apocryphally – to have inspired the old English nursery rhyme *Hickory Dickory Dock*. Beneath the clock is a small door, behind which is a flap. Clergymen would send a cat into the clock's mechanism via this entrance to keep the workings mouse-free. Such vermin control could be the origin of the popular ditty, with its narrative of mice running up and down a striking clock.

'among the most confusing of any church' in England. The red-brick building now hosts a charity for the homeless.

ⓐ 10 Cathedral Yard ① 01392 422396 Ⓦ www.stpetrocks.org.uk
🕒 09.30–17.30 Mon–Fri, 10.00–17.00 Sat, closed Sun

CULTURE

Spacex

With plain, exposed brickwork and stone, and a lot of white and light, this über-modern gallery space offers an unsurprisingly contemporary programme. The projects, exhibitions, events, workshops, talks and activities cater for an inclusively wide audience, feeding on various media and disciplines to do so. Both established and emerging artists take their place in the line-up. Events are also held in the evening. If you're subsequently inspired to turn your own hand to the creative process, the Unearth Gallery next door runs pottery classes

(🖥 www.unearth.picture-box.co.uk). ➌ 45 Preston Street
☎ 01392 431786 🖥 www.spacex.org.uk 🕐 10.00–17.00 Tues–Sat,
closed Sun & Mon

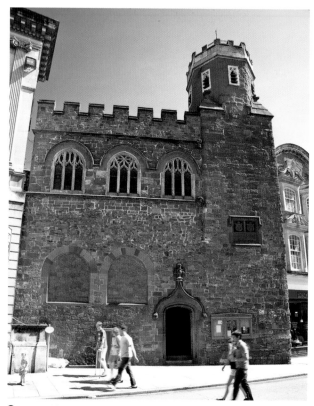

⬛ *St Petrock's dates from the early medieval period*

RETAIL THERAPY

Guildhall Shopping Centre This bills itself as the world's only shopping centre with a 12th-century church at its heart, and part of the attractive building was designed by the same architect who designed Covent Garden in London. Retail giants mingle with smaller stores and independent outlets – head upstairs for the more esoteric shopping options. Rare books, collectibles, classical music, a spa and a juice bar are among the less conventional finds here. Mostly under cover, the centre can offer refuge from the rain. ⓐ Entrances on High Street, North Street and Queen Street ⓣ 01392 201910 ⓦ www.guildhallshoppingexeter.co.uk ⓛ 09.00–18.00 Mon–Wed, 09.00–19.00 Thur–Sat, 10.00–17.00 Sun

Harlequins Shopping Centre Another mix of household names and independent outlets, this shopping centre is a modern and bright mall, entirely inside. A traditional sweets and party emporium, and a Fairtrade Indian clothes and soft-furnishings shop are some of the more unusual outlets. ⓐ Paul Street ⓦ www.harlequinsexeter.co.uk ⓛ 09.00–18.00 Mon–Sat, 10.00–16.00 Sun

High Street Fairly self-explanatory, the High Street is home to all the main names in the retail game. High-end department store House of Fraser, go-to clothing and upmarket food retailer Marks & Spencer, and posh chocolate boutique Thorntons are among the outlets most likely to interest the visitor. ⓐ Northeast of the cathedral

TAKING A BREAK

Refectory £ ❶ Although the quiches, soups, cakes and flapjacks all pass muster, it's the stained-glass windows, strikingly ornate ceiling and general imposing environs that merit a diversion into the cathedral refectory. ⓐ 1 The Cloisters, Cathedral Yard ☏ 01392 285988 ⓦ www.exeter-cathedral.org.uk ⓛ 10.00–16.45 Mon–Sat, closed Sun

Shaker Maker £ ❷ Pink and friendly in equal measure, this jolly, independent takeaway serves bargain baguettes, home-made soup, and a wealth of creative and mouth-watering milk shakes, concocted largely from local ingredients. ⓐ 122 Fore Street ☏ 01392 436717 ⓦ www.shakermaker.biz ⓛ 09.30–17.30 or 18.00 Mon–Sat, 11.00–16.30 Sun

No 21 Cathedral Yard ££ ❸ Warm and inviting café with a reasonably priced breakfast menu, plus sandwiches, salads and light mains. Local specialities, such as warm baguette of West Country sausage accompanied with relish and sautéed onions, rank among the more adventurous options. A good wine and beer selection is available to diners, or you can wash down your lunch with a home-made smoothie or speciality tea. ⓐ 21a Cathedral Yard ☏ 01392 210303 ⓦ www.21cathedralyard-exeter.co.uk ⓛ 09.00–17.00 Mon–Fri, 09.00–18.00 Sat, 10.00–17.00 Sun

Tea on the Green ££ ❹ Housed in a quaint building that dates from 1530, this charming café draws on the British tradition of teatime, the history of tea and coffee, and the influences of the world cuisines that have come to the UK. The extensively tempting menu ranges from all-day breakfasts and snacks to more substantial fare. There's an original bread oven inside, and a glorious cathedral view from the terrace outside. ⓐ 2 Cathedral Close ⓣ 01392 276913 ⓦ www.teaonthegreen.com ⓛ 08.00–18.00 Mon–Sat, 09.00–17.00 Sun

Turk's Head ££ ❺ Once one of the city's oldest pubs, the Turk's Head closed a few years ago and was reborn as part of the Prezzo chain, to the chagrin of pub purists. The pizza and pasta are decent enough, but the main reason to pop in is for the building: this is also the place where Charles Dickens once sipped his beer and people-watched, getting inspiration for some of his memorable characters. ⓐ 202 High Street ⓣ 01392 256680 or 01392 477739 ⓛ 12.00–23.00 Sun–Thur, 12.00–24.00 Fri & Sat

Michael Caines at ABode £££ ❻ Seriously swanky eatery at one of the city's poshest hotels, this place is one of a chain run by a local top chef. Expect ambitious creations, impeccable style – and commensurate prices. Menu highlights include tartlet of Devon quail and roasted breast of guinea fowl. Foodies of means can go for the tasting menu. ⓐ ABode Exeter, Cathedral Yard ⓣ 01392 223638 ⓦ www.michaelcaines.com ⓛ 12.00–14.30 & 18.00–22.00 Mon–Sat, closed Sun

Treasury Restaurant £££ ❼ Classy, stylish and intimate, the Treasury offers a quiet haven for diners looking for a relaxed, upmarket meal (mobile phones are not permitted). The cuisine, which draws extensively on local ingredients, is appropriately sophisticated. ⓐ St Olaves Hotel, Mary Arches Street ⓣ 01392 217736 ⓦ www.olaves.co.uk ⓛ 12.00–14.00 & 19.00–21.00 daily

AFTER DARK

Theatres & cinemas
Barnfield Theatre ❾ Marked by distinctive and quirky fake 'windows', Barnfield Theatre is the base of the Exeter Little Theatre Company, and plays host to performances by both amateur groups and professional troupes. As well as drama, the

◑ *Barnfield Theatre hosts a diverse range of productions*

theatre stages stand-up comedy, puppetry, children's shows, workshops, experimental productions and music, including a full range of tribute bands. Ticket prices are usually reasonable. **ⓐ** Barnfield Road, Southernhay **ⓣ** 01392 270891 **ⓦ** www.barnfieldtheatre.org.uk **ⓛ** Box office: 10.00–16.00 Mon–Fri, 10.00–14.00 Sat, evenings 1 hour before performance commences, closed Sun

The Bike Shed Theatre ❾ Since opening its doors in early 2010, initially as a temporary space for the Particular Theatre (**ⓦ** www.particulartheatre.co.uk), the Bike Shed Theatre has been tasked with hosting the Exeter Fringe Festival. With just 50 seats, it's an undeniably intimate venue, with a retro bar to which the audience can repair after the production. **ⓐ** St Olaves Close, Mary Arches Street **ⓣ** 07880 613869 **ⓦ** www.bikeshedtheatre.co.uk

Corn Exchange ❿ Exeter's largest city-centre venue hosts events ranging from clairvoyance to concerts to comedy, along with plenty of dance evenings to get you practising your moves. **ⓐ** Market Street **ⓣ** 01392 665866 **ⓦ** www.exeter.gov.uk

Exeter Picturehouse ⓫ Housed on the site of a 1930s bus garage, this is one of a select chain of cinemas with an emphasis on independent, art-house, classic films, documentaries and foreign-language films. Live events are hosted here as well, and HD films are now also being shown. **ⓐ** 51 Bartholomew Street West **ⓣ** 0871 902 5730 or 0871 704 2057 **ⓦ** www.picturehouses.co.uk

Around Rougemont

It might be somewhat eclipsed by its larger, more eye-catching and visitor-permitting rival, St Peter's Cathedral, but that should not lead Rougemont Castle to be entirely neglected. The Norman fortress serves as a landmark around which several top Exeter attractions are grouped. This zone, surrounding the northern reaches of the city's Roman wall, is home to a pleasant green area – the adjoining Northernhay and Rougemont gardens – giving it an alluring serenity. The combination of cultural highlights and peaceful parkland means that all but the most breakneck visits should include this part of town, which is just a short walk from the area around the cathedral.

Once again, all the points of interest included here are within minutes' walk of each other. There is a slight risk of getting lost in the large gardens, but their elevation means that views of Central Station or New North Road should help you to regain your bearings.

SIGHTS & ATTRACTIONS

Northernhay Gardens

While their superficial charms alone provide more than enough reason to saunter through this exquisite green plot, Northernhay Gardens are also historically significant, as the oldest public open space in England. Originally established in 1612 as a pleasure walk for the locals, today the gardens have been designated an English Heritage Grade II listed open space. Part of Exeter's Roman wall, as well as the country's only stretch of Saxon town wall, are other inducements for the history buff.

Peaceful and picturesque, the area is dotted with benches on which to sit and listen to the birdsong and enjoy the floral displays. Various Victorian statues lend the gardens an august air, the most recent arrival being Lord Courtenay, who was moved here from Bedford Street in 2010. Other stone luminaries include Stafford Henry Northcote, while E B Stephens' *The Deer Stalker* (1875) is one of the more aesthetically compelling contributions, and the memorial for the Great War the most sobering. Rough-hewn steps to roam, a pretty water feature and a bandstand add to the pleasantness. ⓐ Northernhay Place, between Central Station and Rougemont Gardens ☏ 01392 262630 ⓦ www.exeter.gov.uk ⏱ 07.30–dusk daily

🔺 *The 19th-century Stafford Northcote presides over Northernhay Gardens*

Rougemont Castle

Built at the behest of William the Conqueror just two years after he swept all before him at the Battle of Hastings, the fort was an attempt to gain control over the recalcitrant Exeter, following an 18-day siege. The name is a reference to the red stone from which the fort was originally fashioned, although what is left of that is now in ruins. The castle was rebuilt in Georgian style, and its main parts are now either Grade I or Grade II listed. Housing

THE BIDEFORD WITCH TRIAL

A magpie, a tabby cat, reports of a 'black man', the theft of a doll, nine pinpricks in leather, unexplained illnesses and shaking fits, dubious confessions and hearsay were the evidence that sent the last people in the country to the gallows on the charge of witchcraft. Temperance Lloyd, Mary Trembles and Susannah Edwards hailed from the Devonshire town of Bideford, where their eccentric behaviour aroused the suspicion of the townsfolk and led to accusations of their having practised 'some magical art, sorcery or witchcraft'. They were tried in Exeter and hanged in Heavitree on Friday 25 August 1682, in front of a large crowd. Although further convictions and death sentences were passed against more wretched women, the cases were dropped or the accused pardoned, and in 1736 the crime of witchcraft was taken off the statute books – although public belief in the phenomenon took far longer to subside.

Exeter's legal courts until 2003, the castle was then sold off to a development partnership, which is now pondering how to put it to use. It is hoped that at some point public access may be permitted. Currently it is possible to approach the castle and explore the outside, but few members of the public have ever been in, making it something of an Exeter enigma.

This mysterious atmosphere is palpable at the gatehouse, a dilapidated red-brick building close to the castle entrance. On the garden side of the wall is a plaque in memory of three local women, the last people in England to be hanged for witchcraft (see box opposite). The memorial strikes a sombre note amid the appealing surroundings. ⓐ Castle Street

🔺 *Rougemont Castle stands at the northwest corner of the city walls*

Rougemont Gardens

The original purpose of the gardens adjacent to Rougemont
Castle was to support the military ringwork designed to help
defend the stronghold. This intention seems entirely at odds
with the serenity of the place today. Although in a city centre
and just a short distance from a busy main road, Rougemont
Gardens have the air of a bucolic haven; in the Victorian era the
place was described as a 'perfect sylvan retreat'. For the last
century Rougemont Gardens have been linked to Northernhay
Gardens, and the two can really be treated as one attraction. In
the summer this is the atmospheric setting for the Northcott
Theatre's Shakespeare productions. ⓐ Between Northernhay
Gardens and the Exeter City Central Library ⓣ 01392 262630
ⓦ www.exeter.gov.uk ⓛ Dawn–dusk daily

Underground Passages

Unique, fun and historical, this is a truly brilliant attraction that
will enchant children and entertain adults too. The network of
subterranean tunnels, as deep as 4 m (13 ft) in some places, was
constructed in the 14th century to facilitate the transportation
of fresh water to the cathedral area. The tunnels later provided
shelter during the bombardments of World War II.

Donning hard hats, tourist groups are led around the dank,
narrow passageways, regaled by a guide with tales of rats,
weaponry, volcanic rock and the High Street stores under which
you are currently standing. Buried treasure, escaping nuns and
priests, and a ghost cyclist are among the other legends
associated with the tunnels. Towards the end the route divides,
and there is the option to take a tiny passageway – lower than

1 m (3 ft) at points – back to the start. Don't go dressed in your finery if this appeals, as some crawling and/or stooping is required. These are the only medieval passages in Britain open to visitors and the tour is tremendous fun, but the extreme narrowness of the tunnels makes it unsuitable for claustrophobia sufferers. There's an interesting museum and film to accompany the attraction, both of which are accessible to wheelchair users, although for practical reasons the passages themselves are not. ⓐ 2 Paris Street ① 01392 665887 or 01392 665700 🕒 09.30–17.30 Mon–Sat, 10.30–16.00 Sun (June–Sept & school holidays); 11.30–17.30 Tues–Fri, 09.30–17.30 Sat, 11.30–16.00 Sun, closed Mon (Oct–May); last tour 1 hour before closing ❶ Admission charge

🔺 Relive Exeter's past on the Underground Passages tour

CULTURE

Exeter Phoenix

A lively atmosphere, contemporary space and an eclectic line-up of events and exhibitions make the Phoenix an arts venue of which Exeter can be justly proud. Two galleries on the ground

🔺 *The Exeter Phoenix contemporary arts venue*

floor house rotating exhibits, while upstairs studios host workshops, conferences and the like. Apart from the programmed events, the Phoenix is also a pleasant place to hang out, relax on the terrace, have a bite to eat or go online. ⓐ Bradninch Place, Gandy Street ⓣ 01392 667080 ⓦ www.exeterphoenix.org.uk ⓛ Building: 10.00–23.00 Mon–Sat, 11.00–17.00 Sun (sometimes later for gigs or events); box office: 10.00–20.00 Mon–Sat, 11.30–16.30 Sun

Royal Albert Memorial Museum (RAMM)

Due to reopen after an extensive refit in late 2011, the RAMM looks set to reclaim its status as one of Exeter's premier attractions. The phenomenal one and a half million individual exhibits from around the planet to which the museum lays claim are grouped into antiquities, ethnography, natural history, decorative and fine arts. Until the neo-Gothic building opens its doors once again, exhibits are being farmed out to alternative venues – consult the museum website for further details. ⓐ Queen Street ⓣ 01392 665858 ⓦ www.rammuseum.org.uk ⓛ Closed until late 2011 for a refit; future hours 10.00–17.00 Mon–Sat, closed Sun & bank holidays

RETAIL THERAPY

Gandy Street Charming cobbled Gandy Street has become an enclave of independent businesses, so if you're hoping to pick up some arty souvenirs, atypical jewellery, old vinyl records, clothing or accessories, this is the place to go. ⓦ www.gandyst.co.uk

Princesshay Cathedral views and parts of the city's Roman walls help to beautify the shopping quarter of Princesshay, where over 50 stores vie for your custom. Head to one of seven restaurants, including Carluccio's and Wagamama, for refreshment. 🅰 Bedford Street 🕾 01392 459838 🅦 www.princesshay.com 🕒 09.30–18.00 Mon–Sat, 10.30–16.30 Sun

Sidwell Street Market Fashion, flowers and other sundry buys jostle for your pound at this traditional, open-air market. 🅰 Sidwell Street 🕒 08.30–16.30 Mon–Sat, closed Sun

TAKING A BREAK

This area of the city has a few little gastronomic hubs. There's a cluster of independent cafés on **Catherine Street**, while if you're a chain outlet fan, head to **Princesshay Square**, where Café Rouge, Nando's, Costa and other corporate big guns provide refreshment options.

The businesses operating in **Gandy Street** are proud of their non-corporate, non-chain character, giving the independent-minded a range of choices for eating and drinking.

Coolings £ ⑫ Very cool and laid-back restaurant-bar that is relaxed in the day before moving up a gear for fine dining in the evening. Care and creativity have gone into the main menu, which is cleverly divided into four themes: fire (grilled meat), water (seafood), air (poultry) and earth (vegetarian). 🅰 11 Gandy Street 🕾 01392 434184 🅦 www.coolingsbar.co.uk 🕒 About 10.00–23.30 Mon–Thur, 10.00–24.00 Fri & Sat, 11.00–23.30 Sun

Crêpes Café Gourmandine £ ⑬ Footballers and exquisite culinary taste may not be usual bedfellows, but this place, which opened to much fanfare in late 2009, is the brainchild of Exeter City's French midfielder Bertie Cozic. Drawing on the traditions of both his native Brittany and American-style crêpes, it serves up pancakes, frozen yoghurt and coffee. A few outside tables are on standby for decent weather. ⓐ 14 Catherine Street ① 01392 256428 ① Approximately 09.00–18.00 Mon–Sat, 09.00–17.00 Sun (summer); 10.00–17.00 Mon–Sat, 10.00–16.00 Sun (winter)

The Milkmaid £ ⑭ Its decades-long history of keeping the people of Exeter fed and watered makes The Milkmaid a dependable choice. Split between a self-service coffee bar with freshly baked goodies on the ground floor and table service above, the fare includes English stalwarts spanning breakfast, sandwiches, jacket potatoes and some main meals, including locally caught mackerel with warm potato salad. If it's warm, enjoy an alfresco ice cream. ⓐ 15 Catherine Street ① 01392 277438 ① 08.30–17.00 Mon–Sat, closed Sun

Binelli's ££ ⑮ The wag who had this fabulously fun café decorated with numerous scrawled jokes on the walls (example: Two fish swam into a wall. One said 'dam') has succeeded in setting an exuberant tone that is reflected in the jovial staff. The menu is equally well thought-out, with all the standards such as pizza, pasta, jacket potatoes and sandwiches, a kids' menu, speciality teas and novel juices, as well as 'correttos', or alcoholic coffees. ⓐ 16 Catherine Street ① 01392 499333 ① 08.00–16.30 Mon–Sat, 10.00–16.00 Sun

Innfusion ££ ⓰ This hotel restaurant offers relaxed and friendly service, and a laid-back ambience. Comfort food such as fish and chips and chilli con carne joins lamb, pork, sea bass, pasta, salads and sandwiches on the menu; and the smoked salmon and pesto risotto is a highlight of the specials. The location, just minutes' walk from the bus station, makes Innfusion a convenient filling-up stop if you're on the go, and bar food is served outside meal times. ⓐ Jurys Inn, Western Way ⓣ 01392 312400 or 01392 312333 ⓦ www.exeterhotels.jurysinns.com ⓛ 07.00–10.00 & 18.00–21.30 Mon–Fri, 08.00–10.30 & 18.00–21.30 Sat & Sun

AFTER DARK

Cavern Club ⓱ Although its history is not quite in the same league as its Liverpudlian namesake, Exeter's Cavern Club claims to have put on a remarkable 10,000 bands in its decade of existence. Set up to launch new underground bands, this lively venue was initially about punk rock, but it has gone on to host various names ranging from Coldplay to the Cranberries. The schedule also includes the odd DJ night. ⓐ 83–84 Queen Street ⓣ 01392 495370 ⓦ www.cavernclub.co.uk

John Gandy's ⓲ Pitching itself as friendly, courteous and fun, JG's consists of a bar and restaurant on the ground floor with a galleried cocktail bar up top. Cheap eats are dished up every afternoon from 12.00 to 16.30. Consult the website for events. ⓐ 23 Gandy Street ⓣ 01392 213924 ⓦ www.johngandys.co.uk ⓛ 11.00–24.00 Mon–Thur, 11.00–02.00 Fri & Sat, 12.00–24.00 Sun

Outside the city walls

Moving slightly away from the city centre proper, the third area groups the sights that lie outside the old city wall. Here, the atmosphere is markedly different from that of Exeter's historical heart, giving these attractions something in common despite their varying locations.

The following points of interest can be divided into two clusters: one, the River Exe and The Quay, just to the south of the city centre; and the other, the university, a bus ride or a 15- to 20-minute walk northwards. If you're heading for The Quay, you can readily stroll down from the town centre. The campus-based sights are walkable for the moderately fit, but if you don't fancy expending the effort, or the weather isn't amenable, a bus or taxi will have you there within minutes.

SIGHTS & ATTRACTIONS

Custom House

As this is now a functioning council building, time your visit carefully to make the weekly Custom House Red Coat tour given during the warmer months. It's certainly worth doing, as the knowledgeable guide will bring alive the building's history with fascinating stories of illicit trade and contraband.

The place was built in 1680 as the centrepiece of the new quayside and the bastion of the fight against smuggling, and remained in use by customs authorities right up to 1989. After Exeter lost its wool trade to the mills in the north, canny merchants switched to transporting cargo, such as wines, spirits, timber and oil. The tour takes in the king or queen's pipe – the area where contraband was burned. Theoretically, illegal alcohol imports were poured away under the staircase here, although some may have been retained to whet the palates of the customs officials. To impress the visiting sea captains, cash was lavished on the building, and the ornate ceiling plasterwork – roses, grapes, cherubs – of John Abbott remains one of the eye-catching features. Book the tour at the nearby Quay House Visitor Centre. Even if you can't do the tour, it's worth going along in order to admire the house from the outside.

ⓐ The Quay ⓣ 01392 665700 ⓦ www.exeter.gov.uk ⓛ Tour: 14.00 Sun (Apr–Oct); closed to the public at all other times

🔺 Take a tour of the 17th-century Custom House

The House That Moved

Although it may not, at first glance, differ significantly from the majority of the fine Tudor homes in Exeter, the building on Frog Street has an unusual history. In 1961 the construction of a bypass necessitated the shifting of the entire house from one location to another. The jettied, timber-framed building was hauled on to rollers and inched along the street to its new home. It's not run as a tourist attraction: its new incarnation is as a quaint wedding dress shop. ⓐ Frog Street ⓣ 01392 432643 ⓦ www.pirouettecollection.com

Medieval bridge

The remains of Exeter's Roman city walls are sporadically visible around town (about two-thirds of the original structure are left). However, the size of the medieval bridge makes it worth seeking out. The country's earliest surviving large stone bridge was built at the start of the 13th century, when the River Exe was a lot wider, to cross a waterlogged marsh. Eight and a half arches – or half of the original construction – have survived, although some say that the initial bridge was four times longer than what is left. A key part, rather incongruous to the modern eye, was St Edmund's Church, although the original was replaced in 1833 after a fire; other buildings that bedecked the bridge no longer remain. ⓐ New Bridge Street

The Quay

Leave the city centre behind and wind down at The Quay, a delightful summer destination. What must once have been a thriving whirl of port-related industry is now a place for jogging, walking the dog, feeding the swans and ducks, strolling, taking tea or enjoying a bite to eat. In contrast to the leisurely ambience that presides during the day, after dark things start to look livelier: The Quay is home to some of Exeter's hippest nightspots. ❸ Between the River Exe and the southernmost point of the city wall

◓ This Tudor House was relocated in the 1960s

WEIR-D GOINGS-ON ON THE RIVER

Exeter's economic success was always dependent on its riverside location. Tidal and navigable, the Exe originally facilitated vessel access right up to the city walls themselves. When, at the end of the 13th century, the Countess of Devon had a weir built across the river to support her mills, Exeter was cut off from the sea and its fishing activity was hit hard. The situation was remedied – but only briefly. In 1370 the 9th Earl of Devon put in a new weir, with the result that he could exact huge fees from the boats now obliged to unload at his quay in Topsham. The city fought this shameless piece of chicanery for two and a half centuries before Edward VI finally agreed that the Exe could be reopened. Too late, however – the river had by then silted up. It took Britain's first ship canal in 1563 to reunite Exeter with the English Channel.

Quay House

Now serving primarily as an extremely helpful Visitor Centre, the Quay House is a former storage depot, built in 1680–81 at the same time as Custom House. Besides its tourist advice function, the building is also home to a sort of museum, with displays of local pottery, old maps, information panels and other artefacts. Upstairs the *Exeter – 2,000 Years of History* audiovisual presentation is available on demand. ⓐ The Quay ☎ 01392 271611 ⓦ www.exeter.gov.uk ⏲ 10.00–17.00 daily (Apr–Oct); 11.00–16.00 Sat & Sun, closed Mon–Fri (Nov–Mar)

CULTURE

Bill Douglas Centre

A pleasant 20-minute walk north of the city centre, this shrine to film forms part of the peaceful campus of the University of Exeter, in whose library it is housed. Exhibits such as old magazines and an admission price board chart the history of film from the end of the 18th century, while posters, postcards and paraphernalia of classic productions proliferate. Much of the material is serious and historical, with magic lanterns and optical illusions taking their place alongside exhibits on the role of the auteur and displays on Charlie Chaplin, Alfred Hitchcock and Fritz Lang. But the centre also celebrates the kitsch – of which *Toy Story* figurines, Batman toys, a miniature ET, a

◆ *The Quay House Visitor Centre*

Superman lunchbox, a plastic Jaws, a Fred Astaire and Ginger Rogers card game, and a 1940s *Casablanca* money box give a flavour – which makes the centre fun, even for non-film buffs. There's also a display with details of forthcoming film-related events, such as local film festivals. ⓐ The Old Library, Prince of Wales Road ⓣ 01392 724321 ⓦ www.exeter.ac.uk ⓛ 10.00–17.00 Mon–Fri, closed Sat, Sun & bank holidays ⓝ Bus: D

RETAIL THERAPY

Gift shopping seldom comes with a more pleasant backdrop than **The Quay**. The main retail theme is arty-crafty. It's something of a no-go area for chain outlets, with independent shops the name of the game.

Eclectique A home-furnishings concern that makes its own tables by hand in Devon and also stocks products by must-have names such as Cath Kidston, Emma Bridgewater and Brooklyn Oak. Custom-order some pieces or just pick up a few gifts. Goodwood Cellars, in Cellars 16 & 17 (ⓦ www.goodwoodcellars.co.uk), also handmake eco-friendly furniture. ⓐ Cellars 18 & 23 The Quay ⓣ 01392 250799 ⓦ www.eclectique.co.uk ⓛ 11.00–17.00 daily

Exeter Quay Antiques Centre High-ceilinged, beamed warehouse building where 20 dealers sell books, coins, old postcards, maps and pictures, breakables, vinyl records, toys and other historical wares. It's also home to the charming Riverside Café (see page 77). ⓐ The Quay ⓣ 01392 214180

ⓦ www.exeterquayantiques.co.uk ⏰ 10.00–18.00 daily
(summer); 10.00–17.00 Mon–Fri, 10.00–17.30 Sat & Sun (winter)

Quayside Crafts & Gifts Another cooperative effort, with more
than 50 manufacturers of arts and crafts selling their creations
here. All manner of gift items crowd the store, from cards, clothes
and coins to jewellery and delectable local edibles.
ⓐ 42 The Quay, next to Custom House ☎ 01392 214332
ⓦ www.quaysidecrafts.com ⏰ 10.30–16.30 Mon–Fri, 10.30–17.00
Sat & Sun (Feb–Dec); 10.30–17.00 Sat & Sun, closed Mon–Fri (Jan)

TAKING A BREAK

Bombay Bills ££ ⑲ Replacing the old Havana nightspot, Bombay
Bills serves a choice of Eastern and Western dishes – from
Bombay feasts to burger and fajitas – as well as staging a range
of entertainment, including 'Comedy and Curry' nights. It also
offers Sunday roast lunches. ⓐ 38 Commercial Road, The Quay
☎ 01392 498300 ⓦ www.bombaybills.co.uk ⏰ 17.00–late Thur &
Fri, noon–late Sat & Sun, closed Mon–Wed

The Coffee Cellar ££ ⑳ This is housed in one of the atmospheric
cellars that flank the quayside. Friendly young staff serve up a
selection of goodies, including home-baked cookies, muffins,
cream teas, paninis and baps, which can be washed down with
various teas, coffees and smoothies. Enjoy your refreshments on
the comfy red sofas or outside on the terrace. ⓐ 22 The Quay
☎ 01392 410000 ⓦ www.coffeecellar.co.uk ⏰ 08.30–17.30 daily
(summer); 08.30–16.30 daily (winter)

Mango's ££ ㉑ Sinful smoothies (which come with alcohol) are the most intriguing offering at Mango's, which also boasts 'probably the best coffee in Exeter'. Decorated in bright, bold, purple, red and yellow tones, this spacious eatery serves a wide range of meals, snacks and drinks, and also has a wine list.
ⓐ Kings Wharf, The Quay ❶ 01392 438538
ⓔ thecafeonthequay@aol.com ❶ 10.00–22.00 daily (summer); 10.00–17.00 (winter), weather dependent daily

Riverside Café ££ ㉒ Forming part of the Exeter Quay Antiques Centre (see page 75), this place has a wonderfully genteel atmosphere. It is quaintly done out in low-key blue and white, and prettified with hanging baskets, and the terrace in particular is a lovely spot. The menu covers breakfast, snacks, brunch and lunch, with traditional fare such as ploughman's, jacket potatoes and Devonshire cream teas lining up alongside more exotic offerings such as Thai fishcakes. ⓐ Exeter Quay Antiques Centre, The Quay ❶ 01392 214180
ⓦ www.exeterquayantiques.co.uk ❶ 10.00–18.00 daily (summer); 10.00–17.00 Mon–Fri, 10.00–17.30 Sat & Sun (winter)

On the Waterfront £££ ㉓ The pizzas are what gets everyone talking at On the Waterfront – not surprising considering that they have been endowed with names such as 'Crazy Ass Ring of Fire Extra Hot!'. But the chef also employs local ingredients to come up with dishes such as griddled West Country rib-eye steak. Food – there is a separate bar menu too – is served until 21.00. ⓐ 4–9 The Quay ❶ 01392 210590
ⓦ www.waterfrontexeter.co.uk ❶ 11.00–23.00 daily

AFTER DARK

Theatres

Northcott Theatre After going into administration in early 2010, the Northcott's future was hanging in the balance, but it has now been bought by a company established by the university, ensuring that its first-rate programme of in-house and touring plays, contemporary dance, music and comedy remains secure for the time being at least. The 460-seat venue has hitherto been the city's top theatrical stage, hosting fine actors such as John Nettles, Geraldine James, Celia Imrie and Imelda Staunton. ⓐ Streatham Campus, University of Exeter, Stocker Road ⓣ 01392 493493 ⓦ www.exeternorthcott.co.uk ⓝ Bus: D, 55A

Clubs & pubs

Lemon Grove Being a university concern the gigs here are term time only, but are open to all comers. Music-wise, it's a fairly mixed bag, with a studenty vibe. ⓐ Cornwall House, University of Exeter ⓣ 01392 425309 ⓝ Bus: D, 55A

Prospect Inn This modernised 17th-century pub enjoys a great quayside location and offers food until 21.00. Trivia buffs may like to know that it served as a location for the 1970s BBC shipping drama *The Onedin Line*. ⓐ The Quay ⓣ 01392 273152 ⓦ www.heavitreebrewery.co.uk ⓛ 10.00–23.00 Sun–Thur, 10.00–24.00 Fri & Sat

ⓞ *The harbour at Exmouth*

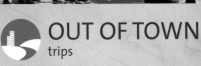

OUT OF TOWN
trips

Dartmoor National Park

Southern England's greatest wilderness, Dartmoor seethes with the rugged possibilities of nature and more than a hint of mystery and mythology. Peppering its wild moorland, tors and rivers are ancient sites and relics, and a wealth of flora and fauna, including its famous ponies. Apart from simply taking in the majestic and brooding atmosphere that inspired Sir Arthur Conan Doyle to pen *The Hound of the Baskervilles*, there are plenty of ways to pass the time, including hiking, cycling, climbing, horse riding (or indeed pony trekking) and white-water rafting.

GETTING THERE

When you're talking about an undeveloped open space the size of Dartmoor, the most convenient method of getting there and around is in your own or a hire car. However, many people are reluctant to drive out of environmental concern, and from Exeter it's perfectly possible to do Dartmoor by public transport, with a little advance planning. Useful bus services in this respect include the 82, X9, X10, X11, X38 and 173; expect the journey to take at least 40 minutes, maybe an hour. If you'd rather someone else made the arrangements, organised day trips to Dartmoor can be taken from Exeter.

SIGHTS & ATTRACTIONS

The main appeal of Dartmoor is taking in the savage beauty of the landscape, perhaps atop a pony or pulling on hiking boots for a ramble. But there are also some more specific attractions to visit.

Dartmoor Prison Museum

Tales of notorious inmates past, a macabre flogging frame and ingeniously improvised contraband, such as a knife made out of matchsticks, will entertain visitors to this unusual museum, which asserts a dark fascination. Genial staff are on hand to provide interested parties with more details. ⓐ Princetown, next to the prison ⓣ 01822 892130 ⓦ www.dartmoor-prison.co.uk ⓛ 09.30–12.30 & 13.30–16.30 Mon–Thur & Sat, 09.30–12.30 & 13.30–16.00 Fri & Sun; last admission 30 minutes before closing ⓝ Bus: 82, 98; 272 (summer only) ⓘ Admission charge

△ *Tarns and tors: Dartmoor National Park*

Museum of Dartmoor Life

Charting the demanding lives of Dartmoor's residents, the three floors of exhibits bear tribute to man's ingenuity in the face of inclement nature. 3 West Street, Okehampton 01837 52295 www.museumofdartmoorlife.eclipse.co.uk 10.15–16.30 Mon–Sat, closed Sun (Easter–Oct); opening hours vary in winter Bus: 118, 179, 318, 510, X9; Train: Okehampton Admission charge

TAKING A BREAK

Tors Restaurant ££ With a creative take on traditional fare – where red onion, Sharpham brie and spinach frittata rub shoulders with steak and chips – the restaurant at this over-two-centuries-old inn offers a sumptuous atmosphere and first-class food. Two Bridges Hotel, Princetown 01822 890581 www.twobridges.co.uk Evenings only, bar food available during the day Bus: 82, 98; 272 (summer only)

Gidleigh Park £££ If you have serious cash to splash, there are few better places to splash it than at this two-Michelin-starred country hotel restaurant, another one under the auspices of Exeter chef Michael Caines. Contemporary European fare at its most inventive: think tartlet of quails' eggs and frogs' legs with crayfish. Chagford 01647 432367 www.gidleigh.com 12.30–14.00 & 19.00–21.00 daily

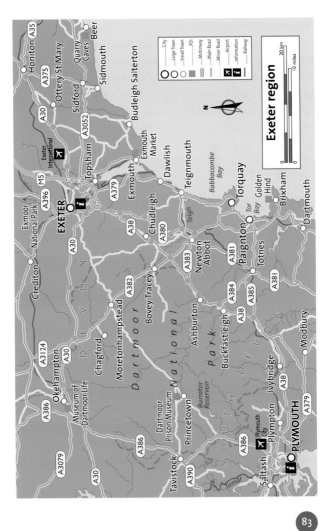

South Devon coast

Whatever type of beachgoer you are, the South Devon coast has a spot to suit, from genteel, olde-worlde seaside towns that hark back to bygone eras to cheap and cheerful bucket-and-spade resorts and low-key getaways – not to mention the English Riviera. Although Mediterranean balminess cannot be guaranteed, the sun graces the county with its presence fairly often, and the relaxing coastal atmosphere makes this area a pleasant interlude in your urban Exeter experience.

GETTING THERE

Various buses shuttle between Exeter and the resorts covered here. Journey times are in the region of an hour, depending on the individual resort and bus route. Exmouth is unusual in having its own train station, between half and three-quarters of an hour away from Exeter.

SIGHTS & ATTRACTIONS

Beer

Untouched by the tourism that permeates many seaside resorts, Beer is pretty and remains wonderfully authentic. The tiny fishing village still relies on piscatorial pursuits for its living, and vividly coloured vessels adorn the beach. The catch of the day doesn't get much fresher than on Sea Hill, the sheer approach to the beach where you can pick up lunch or dinner recently plucked from the sea. Its tortuous inlets made Beer

◆ *Brixham's colourful seafront*

fertile smuggling territory, and the caves that were at the heart of the contraband trade make a diverting excursion. Beer Quarry Caves  Quarry Lane  01297 680282  www.beerquarrycaves.fsnet.co.uk  10.00–17.00 daily (Easter–Sept); 11.00–16.00 daily (Oct); other times by appointment  Bus: X53, X54, 52A (to nearby Seaton), 899  Admission charge

Brixham

Titivated by the pastel-coloured hilltop buildings that give on to the bay, Brixham is a characterful, jolly resort, centring on the actual-size *Golden Hind* replica, based on the ship that Sir Francis Drake used to circumnavigate the globe between 1577 and 1580. **Golden Hind**  Brixham Harbour  01803 856223  www.goldenhind.co.uk  10.00–16.00 daily (mid-Feb–Oct); hours vary in winter and during school holidays  Bus: 12, 12A, 22, 24, 66 (from local destinations); Coach: Exeter

Exmouth

Breathe in the tempting aroma of fish and chips and revel in the atmosphere of this traditional English seaside resort. The evergreen pleasures of the coast, such as the seafront promenade and elegant period terraces, combine with the modern thrills of watersports to bring new generations of holidaymakers to what has been described as the county's oldest coastal resort. The market yields some top bargains. **Exmouth Market**  The Strand  01395 264347  09.00–17.00 Mon–Sat (all year), plus 10.00–16.00 Sun (Aug)  Bus: 56, 57; Train: Exmouth

Sidmouth

Close to 500 listed buildings make Sidmouth one of the more well-to-do resorts on Devon's south coast. It was ever thus: aristocrats lived it up here in the 1800s, and the architectural legacy is evident in fine Regency buildings, wrought iron, crenellations and numerous period features. The esplanade is popular for constitutionals – interludes can be taken on the deckchairs dotted along its length – and there are plenty of olde-worlde shops with traditional wares. If you're coming for the beach, be warned that high tide completely covers the sand, leaving just shingle exposed. Ⓝ Bus: 52A, 52B; 387 (Sat only), 379 (Sun and bank holidays only)

Torquay

It will always be famous as the location of Basil Fawlty's fictional disaster of a hotel, but the modern Torquay is trying hard to reinvent itself under the 'English Riviera' banner. A benign microclimate, plenty of green space, white villas and palm trees all do their bit to boost the appeal, as does the Victorian pier. Devon's third-largest town, the place has a markedly different feel from its neighbours. A large contingent of foreign visitors (many of whom are students) confers on it a cosmopolitanism somewhat at odds with its resolute Englishness. Ⓝ Bus: 12A, X80, 111, 112 (from local destinations); Coach: Exeter; Train: Torquay

TAKING A BREAK

Brophy's ££ Genial service and a warm atmosphere make a stop at Brophy's a pleasure. Light lunches and snacks, including

sandwiches and baguettes, join tempting treats such as home-made cakes and cream teas. Linger over a newspaper as you eat.
ⓐ 6 High Street, Sidmouth ⓣ 01395 578998 ⓛ 09.30–16.30 Mon–Sat, 10.00–16.00 Sun ⓝ Bus: 52A, 52B, 157, 382, 387, 899

AFTER DARK

Orange Tree £££ This upmarket restaurant carefully fashions local ingredients into fine examples of national and continental cuisine. Dishes such as risotto of asparagus with Devon Blue cheese, 'Orange Tree' tournedos with foie gras, and king scallops with smoked salmon convey a flavour of the ambition and style.
ⓐ 14–16 Parkhill Road, Torquay ⓣ 01803 213936
ⓦ www.orangetreerestaurant.co.uk ⓛ 19.00–late Mon–Sat, closed Sun ⓝ Bus: 11, 12, 31, 32, 34, X46, 60, 51, 64, 65, X80, X81, 100, 110, 111, 112

ⓞ *The* Golden Hind *replica at Brixham*

PRACTICAL
information

Directory

GETTING THERE

By air

Exeter's location on England's southwest peninsula makes it something of a trek from much of the UK, but the very conveniently positioned airport has put the city within much easier reach of the rest of the country. Several domestic airports have direct, scheduled flights to Exeter – currently Aberdeen, Belfast, Edinburgh, Glasgow, Guernsey, Jersey, Leeds-Bradford, Manchester, Newcastle and Norwich – all with low-cost carrier Flybe.

Exeter Airport Ⓦ www.exeter-airport.co.uk

Flybe Ⓦ www.flybe.com

Many people are aware that air travel emits CO_2, which contributes to climate change. You may be interested in the possibility of lessening the environmental impact of your flight through the charity **Climate Care** (Ⓦ www.jpmorganclimatecare.com), which offsets your CO_2 by funding environmental projects around the world.

By rail

Most intercity trains arrive at Exeter St David's. There are direct trains from London Paddington, which ordinarily take just over two hours (London Waterloo also has a much slower service), and from Birmingham New Street (two and a half hours). From most other cities, however, you'll have to change trains (although Manchester, for example, does have the odd direct service). Several websites – either specific to the region or with nationwide coverage – can be used to reserve your ticket before travelling, giving you access to cheaper fares.

First Great Western Ⓦ www.firstgreatwestern.co.uk

National Rail Ⓦ www.nationalrail.co.uk

The Trainline Ⓦ www.thetrainline.com

By road

Long-distance coaches also serve the city. From London the journey time is likely to be in the region or upwards of four and a half hours. Coaches in the UK are usually cheaper (but slower) than trains.

Exeter Bus Station ⓐ Paris Street ⓣ 01392 427711

Megabus Ⓦ www.megabus.com/uk

National Express Ⓦ www.nationalexpress.com

If your Exeter visit is part of a wider regional trip, especially one that's going to take in Dartmoor or multiple towns, the use of a car can be handy. From London the journey by car takes about three and a half hours.

If you wish to hire a vehicle for your stay, car-hire outlets can be found at the airport and in town, with a cluster on the Marsh Barton Trading Estate, accessible via Alphington Road (Ⓜ Bus: B, Park & Ride). If a bicycle is more your thing, try Saddles & Paddles (see page 20).

Avis Ⓦ www.avis.co.uk

Budget Ⓦ www.budget.co.uk

Europcar Ⓦ www.europcar.co.uk

Hertz Ⓦ www.hertz.co.uk

National Ⓦ www.nationalcar.co.uk

Sixt Ⓦ www.sixt.co.uk

Thrifty Ⓦ www.thrifty.co.uk

HEALTH, SAFETY & CRIME
Health

For non-urgent medical help, contact NHS Direct (**☎** 0845 4647) or you can go online (**ⓦ** www.nhsdirect.nhs.uk).

Emergency Dental Service **ⓐ** 3rd Floor, Royal Devon & Exeter Hospital (Heavitree), Gladstone Road **☎** 01392 405700

Royal Devon & Exeter Hospital (emergencies) **ⓐ** Barrack Road **☎** 01392 411611 **ⓦ** www.rdehospital.nhs.uk

Safety & crime

Exeter's crime stats do not differ significantly from the national average. However, late-night revelry and the rare persistent beggar can make the visitor feel slightly ill at ease. As well as avoiding the neighbourhood of pubs and nightclubs at 'chucking-out time', all the usual safety advice applies: keep your valuables securely about your person, avoid wandering around alone in dark and deserted areas late at night, and be aware of anyone standing too close at a cash point (ATM) and similar. In an emergency, dial 999 or the international number 112.

Exeter Police Station **ⓐ** Heavitree Road **☎** 08452 777444 (for non-emergencies only) **ⓦ** www.devon-cornwall.police.uk

TOILETS

If a public toilet does not present itself when the need strikes, many people pop into the nearest pub or hotel, either throwing themselves on the mercy of the staff or just discreetly nipping in. Attractions should all have well-maintained toilets. Train and bus stations sometimes levy a charge for the use of their conveniences.

CHILDREN

Exeter's main highlights are not particularly child-oriented – with the exception of the Underground Passages, which go down a storm with all but the most timid young visitor. Slightly older children may enjoy the RAMM (when it reopens), the Phoenix and the Bill Douglas Centre, or some of the watersports, while the quayside with its swans and ducks is a fun place for younger family members. The wider area, taking in Dartmoor and the beach resorts, promises superb times for kids.

TRAVELLERS WITH DISABILITIES

Its leisurely pace makes Exeter one of the UK's less daunting cities if your mobility is restricted. While some sights – the tunnels of the Underground Passages, for example – are unavoidably off-limits, others – including St Peter's Cathedral (where a wheelchair and touch model are provided), Exeter Picturehouse, Spacex, The Quay and Princesshay – make an effort to ensure that they can welcome disabled visitors. Swathes of pedestrianised areas also help. The Exeter and Essential Devon website (ⓦ www.exeterandessentialdevon.com) gives information on the accessibility situation for individual attractions.

FURTHER INFORMATION

Amenable staff at the Quay House Visitor Centre will go out of their way to help you. The city council website (ⓦ www.exeter.gov.uk) also has details of a host of attractions. **Quay House Visitor Centre** ⓐ The Quay ⓣ 01392 271611 ⓦ www.exeter.gov.uk ⓛ 10.00–17.00 daily (Apr–Oct); 11.00–16.00 Sat & Sun, closed Mon–Fri (Nov–Mar)

ACKNOWLEDGEMENTS

The photographs in this book were taken by Stephen Varty for Thomas Cook Publishing, to whom the copyright belongs, except for the following: iStockphoto pages 5 (K Stuart), 13 (Nickos), 17 (Bruce Block), 19 (Rolling Earth), 37, 50, 70 (Mrtom UK), 46 (Chrislastphoto), 79 (Garnhamphotography), 81 (Blackbeck); Shutterstock page 9 (Jeff Banke)

Project editor: Penny Isaac
Copy editor: Caroline Churton
Proofreaders: Penny Isaac & Lucilla Watson
Layout: Trevor Double
Indexer: Karolin Thomas

AUTHOR BIOGRAPHY

Debbie Stowe is a freelance journalist, travel writer and author. She has written over a dozen non-fiction and travel books, specialising in Indian Ocean and Eastern European destinations. Her writing also covers the natural world, film, human rights, and cultural and social issues. She lives in Bucharest with her partner.

Send your thoughts to
books@thomascook.com

- **Found a great bar, club, shop or must-see sight that we don't feature?**
- **Like to tip us off about any information that needs a little updating?**
- **Want to tell us what you love about this handy little guidebook and more importantly how we can make it even handier?**

Then here's your chance to tell all! Send us ideas, discoveries and recommendations today and then look out for your valuable input in the next edition of this title.

Email the above address (stating the title) or write to:
pocket guides Series Editor, Thomas Cook Publishing, PO Box 227, Coningsby Road, Peterborough PE3 8SB, UK.